UNDOING RACISM

A PHILOSOPHY OF INTERNATIONAL SOCIAL CHANGE

THE PEOPLE'S INSTITUTE FOR SURVIVAL AND BEYOND

Dedicated to Training with
Intelligence and Integrity —
with Values and Vision

Second Edition

RONALD CHISOM
and
MICHAEL WASHINGTON

The People's Institute Press

Volume One

Published by The People's Institute Press 1997
The first edition was published by the Afro-American
Studies Program at Northern Kentucky University.

For more information, write to:

Ronald Chisom/Michael Washington
The People's Institute for Survival and Beyond
1444 North Johnson Street
New Orleans, LA 70116

ISBN   0 - 9653305 - 1 - 6

Dedicated to

🐟 **Dr. James Norman Dunn** 🐟

1932-1989

Acknowledgements

A portion of this manuscript was translated into Japanese and published in *Human Rights,* a journal of the Buraku Kaiho Kenkyujo, in March and April, 1996. We would like to thank The Association To Stop Racism Against Blacks, particularly the Arita family, for initiating the project and also the Kenkyujo for making this work available for the Japanese audience. We would also like to thank Professor Yasue Kuwahara for her careful reading of the manuscript; The People's Institute for Survival and Beyond and Northern Kentucky University for the publication and dissemination of this work and the first edition of this manuscript. Special thanks must also be extended to the core trainers of The Institute, whose contributions to the development of both the ethical assumptions and the training curriculum has been invaluable to this work. In this regard, we are indebted to the Reverends David Billings and Daniel Buford, Ms. Diana Dunn and Ms. Barbara Major.

Other individuals who have supported the work of The People's Institute and are worthy of acknowledgement include:

Dr. Mary Abell, Shadia Alvarez, Irma Bartholemy, Joe Barndt, Anne Braden, Stephanie Burrows-Stafford, Jyaphia Christos-Rodgers, Sheila Collins, Gerry Conroy, Dan Debessay, Evelyn Dettling, Vergie Encalade, Dr. Donald T. Erwin, Johnny Holloway, Mel Hoover, Jean Kirgess, Theresa Lenear, Arnette Lewis, Sharon

Martinas, Marcos McPeek, Mary Priniski, William Quigley, Ray Santigo, Louise Derman-Sparks, Les Schmidt, Pat Trammel, C.T. Vivian, Mary Welsh, Esther Yazee, Fiettana Yungai, and Brenda Zook. Those who serve as resource trainers with The People's Institute should also be acknowledged for their dedication to the ideals of the organization. Such people include: Margery Freeman, Muhjah Hasan, James Hayes, David Larsen, John Morrin, Maria Reinat-Pumarejo, Dr. Kimberley Richards and Monica Walker.

Finally, several groups have been instrumental in the support and encouragement of The People's Institute's work. Such groups include: the members of the board of the directors of The People's Institute for Survival and Beyond, the St. Thomas Resident Council, the Treme Community Improvement Association, The Fisherman and Concerned Citizens Association (of Plaquemine's Parish), the H. U. M. A. N. (Help Us Make A Nation) Network, and the Southern Organizing Committee for Social and Economic Justice (S.O.C.).

FORWARD

With the mission of building a multi-racial, anti-racist liberation movement throughout the United States, the People's Institute for Survival and Beyond, referred to hereafter as the People's Institute, has as its goal to develop accountable leadership equipped with the values, knowledge, and skills to work effectively towards the undoing of racism. It is important to note here that the adjectives, multi-racial and anti-racist, have very specific meanings. Multi-racial denotes a group's racial composition which suggests more than two races are involved. On the other hand, the term anti-racist speaks to the intent of the multi-racial group which is to work toward the undoing of racism. The People's Institute views racism as a structural/political reality that functions to maintain all of the other forms of oppression. From this perspective, the movements to eliminate classism, sexism, homophobialism, or any other oppressive "ism" cannot succeed unless the undoing of racism is a primary focus of such movements. For as long as people are oppressed because of their color, the elimination of the other "isms" (if possible) would only benefit white people; yet those of color who are poor, or who are women, or who are homosexuals, etc., will continue to face their particular forms of oppression in addition to facing racism. What is more, the privileges ascribed to whites in a racist society oftentimes prohibit white activists from developing multi-racial and anti-racist organizations or from building effective coalitions with people of color. Hence, the other "isms" are unsuccessfully attacked because of the ineffectiveness of white groups in discarding racist attitudes and behaviors from their approaches to organizing. It is for these reasons that the People's Institute takes the position that racism is not just another issue but the most critical barrier to building a true multi-racial, anti-racist liberation movement in the United States.

We therefore assume that it is essential to move forward with a different approach to organizing and educating people: one which allows them to see the interrelationships between their issues and the undoing of racism. To this end the People's Institute, in its approach to training, recognizes certain principles that are critical to the development of the kinds of people's organizations that are needed today. These principles include the indepth understanding of racism, militarism, culture, and history as well as accountability, the internal dynamics of leadership development and networking.

Our methods of implementing the above principles consist of four types of workshops and training sessions which include the Core Workshop, Advanced Training Sessions, specialized Workshops, and Crisis/Technical Assistance Workshops. The Core workshp is a two and a half day training session generally beginning Friday evening and ending late Sunday afternoon. This is our entry level workshop that sets the "context for organizing" as desribed in this manuscript and then focuses on the specific area of concern that is agreed upon by the trainers and participants through an intensive process of contract negotiations (establishing an agreement for a productive working relationship). The Advanced Training Session is an indepth four day training offered each year and aimed at selected participants. Completion of the entry level Core Workshop is a prerequisite to be considered to be invited. Most of the participants are people representing organizations we worked with and have maintained some degree of follow-up throughout the years. Upon invitation, the People's Institute trainers will offer Specialized Workshops focusing on specific issues of community concern that have been jointly identified by the community and the trainers. Many of the skills needed in these workshops involve some of the same ones gained in the above sessions. An example of such skills could include military counter-recruitment, building a multi-racial network, or undoing racism, etc. The Crisis Intervention/Technical Training workshops are designed to help with organizational development, conflict management, personal development, internal group relations, etc.

All workshop formats are set within the context of the seven principles. We have also built into the program a process to put groups we work with on a local level into a networking relationship with other groups that have similar needs, concerns, and a shared vision for change. This allows otherwise dependent people to resource each other and become more empowered through the development of a sense of unity and interdependency. This aspect of the training has been one of the more exciting and successful components of our work.

The skills taught by the People's Institute, once the context is established, include such basics as the nuts and bolts of creating and maintaining grassroots organizations; recruiting and keeping members; conducting effective meetings; setting up and working with the boards of directors; keeping the membership and leadership accountable to each other; setting realistic goals and developing effective strategies for winning victories; understanding the differences between organizing and mobilizing and learning how to deal with rather than avoid internal conflict.

The origins of the need for this type of training began in the 1960s and 70s when the founders of our organization, who were unknown to each other at the time, were seeking advanced training in community organizing. The similarity in their experiences was that all of their training was done by whites who were unaware of the significance of culture and/or the adverse influence of white cultural values when organizing within the context of a racist society. The training therefore focused completely on learning the technical/mechanical skills of organizing which were simply not enough to be effective in doing anti-racist work. What was needed to strengthen the development of the technical/mechanical skills was a humanistic code of ethics. Our hope is that this work will address that need.

Table of Contents

INTRODUCTION

I The Chisom Case

A headline in the August 27, 1992 issue of *The Times Picayune*, the major newspaper in New Orleans, Louisiana, reads, "Settlement may seat black justice." The article goes on to describe the process by which "the Louisiana Supreme Court could have its first black justice* as a result of a settlement . . . that sought a majority black district in New Orleans for the high court." The issue has to do with the fact that in the entire history of the United States of America in general and the State of Louisiana in particular, there has never been an African American (black person) to sit on Louisiana's Supreme Court.

This appalling reality is in part responsible for the disproportionate number of African Americans locked up in Louisiana's prisons and for the longer sentences they receive when compared to their white counterparts. Even more shocking is the historic reality that African Americans have lived in New Orleans, Louisiana even before Thomas Jefferson, the third president of the United States, purchased the Louisiana Territory from France in 1803. Back then, a great number of these

---

Note: "black" is used synonymously with "African American." Whites tend not to capitalize "black" as they do all other ethnic groups which causes Black Americans to prefer to be called African Americans.

African peoples had been forced into slavery by whites who controlled the legal system. As a result of the American South losing the Civil War in 1865, the enslaved African Americans were freed but were never permitted to live free from white prejudice and white institutional discrimination. Indeed, a full one hundred years after the Civil War, African Americans were still systematically denied the right to vote. Because of this, they struggled to get the federal government to pass the Voting Rights Act in 1965 which prohibits diluting the strength of the African American vote.

Despite the passage of the Voting Rights Act in 1965, the whites who controlled the legal system in Louisiana continued to deny African Americans the right to elect an African American to the state's Supreme Court by cleverly diluting their voting strength. This was accomplished by combining a majority African American voting district with three other predominantly white districts thereby guaranteeing that whites would always be able to out-vote African Americans and elect whites to the Supreme Court.

It was this structured, institutionalized racist political arrangement that resulted in the challenge to the system of electing state Supreme Court Justices. In what came to be known as the "Chisom Case," this legitimatized system of maintaining white supremacy in Louisiana's voting process of electing Supreme Court justices is now being challenged and by the year 2000 it should finally be dismantled. For, in 1991 the U.S. Supreme Court said all judicial elections come under the Voting Rights Act, which bars dilution of black voting strength and since then a settlement has been reached in Louisiana which calls for statewide reapportionment of the Supreme Court districts in 1998, to take effect in 2000. This is an example of "undoing racism."

The "Chisom Case" gets its name from Ronald

Chisom, the lead plaintiff who filed suit against the state of Louisiana. Ronald Chisom, a co-author of this monograph, is also one of the founders and co-director of an organization called The People's Institute for Survival and Beyond (referred to hereafter as The People's Institute). The People's Institute is a national organization of multi-racial, anti-racist experienced community organizers and educators dedicated to building an effective movement for social change.

From the perspective of the People's Institute, the focal point of social change is the challenge of undoing racism and all of its manifestations. The People's Institute views racism as a very specific form of oppression. Racism is different from nationalism, classism, sexism, ethnocentrism or any other "ism." It is also different from prejudice. When a society is structured to oppress people on the basis of race the intention is to maintain unequitable social relations whereby a superior race dominates inferior ones. Since the inferior races are denied adequate representation in the courts, the people who are members of an inferior race are not intended to experience justice. Hence, racism is not merely an intellectual concept. It is the normal experience of living in an inequitable and unjust society. Since a community can only achieve equity through the power of its organized strength, it is important that we begin our discussion of racism by placing it in the context of a philosophy of community organizing that seeks to bring about equitable social relations. Let us now examine the concept of undoing racism as a philosophy of equity and justice.

UNDOING RACISM:
THE PHILOSOPHICAL BASIS
FOR AN EQUITABLE AND JUST SOCIETY

II Undoing Racism:

The Philosophical Basis for an Equitable and Just Society

Undoing racism as our philosophy of equity and justice is based on five basic philosophical assumptions. By "our philosophy" we mean the system of values by which our organization lives. The system of values which informs the work of the People's Institute is what we refer to as the ethics of undoing racism.

As an ethical way of life, the philosophy of undoing racism is undergirded by five basic assumptions. *First, it assumes that to be normal does not necessarily mean to be healthy.* To be normal simply means to conform to the norms of a given society. When a society is structured on the basis of race, each member of society is given a racial designation and is expected to conform to the norms of its designated racial group. Whites, for instance, are expected to conform to having more privileges than non-whites and would be considered deviant from white societal norms if they would risk their privileges or their lives to dedicate themselves to the struggle for Black equality (or for that matter, the equality of any non-white race).

While it is quite normal for whites to conform to having more privileges than non-whites, it is not healthy for either the white individual or the society at large. Like the slavemaster who could not sleep at night unless his gun was close by his bedside, normal whites in today's society often suffer high-anxiety when policies dictate that adjustments be made to insure racial equity. This is not a healthy state of existence because when the norm is for whites to deny others equitable treatment on the basis of race, the society will experience an inordinate amount of racial hostility, violence and crime.

Likewise, when non-whites conform to the norms of the inferior race to which they have been designated, their normal patterns of behavior should not be confused with a healthy state of existence. Because their racial roles dictate that they be inferior to whites, the "white way" is often viewed by them as being "better" than their own ways. For instance, it is normal for such persons to undercut the economic stability of their own communities by spending their money in white-owned stores rather than supporting the businesses which are owned and operated by members of their own race. Another example is that far too many Black children still prefer white dolls over black ones. What is more, the self-inflicted violations of humanity in the way of sexual abuse, assaults and homicides become commonplace and are perceived as normal activities within the context of many non-white communities. *It must therefore be assumed that when a society is structured on the basis of race, conformity to the norms of racial roles maintains both inequitable treatment and pathological relations.*

The second basic assumption which undergirds the ethics of undoing racism is that *effective community organizing must be consistently taking place by community organizers who live by a commitment to sound social/moral ethics.* Such organizers must possess four essential qualities. First, they must be intelligent and be dedicated to training community leaders to acquire their insights. As intelligent beings they are able to distinguish justice from injustice. They have a basic understanding of the fact that the transformation of society can only take place when people engage in the process of transforming their own lives. They know that every individual, including themselves, has a responsibility in the transformational process. They also know that the development of ordinary people into accountable leaders is a prerequisite for community empowerment.

Another quality essential for effective community organizers is integrity. It is not enough to know of one's responsibility to community empowerment; one must be willing to be held accountable to a constituency and educate others to value and create accountable relations with each other. Without accountability, equity is not guaranteed, yet far too many people claiming to be community organizers are lacking in this essential quality; the quality of possessing integrity which makes one willing to be held accountable.

A third quality of such community organizers is the possession of humanistic values. Such values are expressed by a profound appreciation of human culture. In a society that dehumanizes on the basis of race, the community organizer recognizes human culture as the life blood of the oppressed people and seeks to use the peoples' culture as an organizing tool to help them gain a sense of their transformative power.

A fourth quality possessed by effective community organizers is a sense of vision. The vision is to live in an equitable environment. While such a vision may appear a bit far-fetched to the average person, it is the organizer's effectiveness at developing accountable leaders that sustains vision by providing her/him with a sense of hope. While the lack of vision has caused many organizers to "burn-out," those who possess this invaluable quality become the models of the society they hope to create by maintaining accountable relationships with their developing leaders and with the institutions that impact their communities. *In short, this assumption suggests that an equitable environment is sustained by consistent community organizing carried out by ethically sound organizers who are dedicated to training with intelligence and integrity; with values and vision.*

While the above four qualities address our second assumption and speak to the ethical character of a community organizer, the third basic assumption pertinent to attaining equity is that the *organizers must have a clear understanding of the process of disempowerment in order to be effective in helping people to gain a sense of their power.* This assumption is an important one because many people who carry the title of community organizer operate under the false belief that winning issues is the purpose of their existence. This method of organizing invariably leads to the syndrome of reacting to a myriad of issues and emotional crises. Organizers of this type often become issue hoppers especially when funders define and fund the issues they hop to. Generally speaking, even when organizers of this sort win issues that were responses to emotional crises, the community remains unorganized and no new leadership tends to emerge from the effort. To be more effective organizers must view their work as a means to recruit and develop leadership in the struggle. As long as the race-structured society exists, there will be the need for an effective on-going struggle for racial equity. Community organizers must understand this fundamental point and approach the organizing effort as a process of developing leadership for the long run. Regardless of whether the issue is health care, housing, homelessness, etc., the effectiveness of the community organizer begins with the basic question of "What is the process by which my constituency has been disempowered?" In other words, the effective organizer seeks to understand the structural forces which function to disempower the people, then use the issue as a vehicle by which to help the people gain a sense of their power and take greater control of their lives. By seeking to understand the process by which people become disempowered, the effective organizer avoids blaming the people for their disadvantaged condition. Instead, the organizer teaches the constituency group how to analyze institutional power and to understand the effects of that power on poor people and their communities.

For instance, the organizer whose constituency group is working on the issue of public housing must make certain that the group has an understanding of how the housing industry functions as an oppressive institution. When this happens, the group emerges with a general understanding of why the government built the projects for whites in the 1930s. The group will also know how the G.I. Bill allowed whites to escape the projects but kept African Americans trapped in the inner-city because of government programs such as the 235 Homeownership program claiming not to have the money to lend to them. The organizer will also make certain that the group has a thorough understanding of specific vocabulary words which are important to the analysis. Such words could be; racial covenants, redlining, blockbusting, steering, etc.

The power analysis will also enable the group to understand the interconnectedness between the institution of public housing and other institutions which function to disempower the poor. For instance, the group will become more conscious of why their public educational system insists on enforcing a neighborhood school policy which maintains racially segregated, inferior black schools. The interconnection between housing and redlining policies used by financial institutions, insurances companies, etc., helps the constituency group to understand the process of devaluing an entire community by labeling all of its residents "high risks." By effectively engaging in this process, the organizer brings the constituency group to the awareness that people are not poor because they lack adequate services from the housing authority or any other service providers. They are poor because they lack the power to control their lives. It becomes the task of the community organizer to help the people transform their behavior to conform to patterns of having greater control of the resources that improve the quality of their lives.

Even after knowing all of the information of how institutions function to disempower a community, the people are still not necessarily willing to challenge the institutions to attain equitable treatment. This is because the process of disempowerment has caused those who have been disempowered to internalize their inferiority. The organizer is fully aware of this process as both a class and race phenomenon and teaches it to the constituency group. Thus, the constituents become conscious of both the importance of organizing across racial lines and the tremendous difficulty in being effective at achieving this task. They learn that because poverty is a structural aspect of a capitalistic society, many people, by necessity, are conditioned by the institutions of society to conform to being poor. The conditioning process consists of such experiences as: chronic unemployment, a lack of access to quality education and health care, dependency on governmental assistance programs, and a host of other experiences which subordinate poor people to the system.

Because of the similarities of living in poverty by poor people of all races, it would seem logical for an orga-

21

nizer to attempt to organize the poor across racial lines. However, this is in fact a monumental challenge because of the belief among poor whites that because they are white, they should be "more better off" than the minority races. This belief is an expression of the ideology of racism which functions to keep the entire class of poor people divided along racial lines. As long as poor whites are unwilling to organize with poor non-whites to improve the conditions of all, the existence of economic and racial inequity will continue to prevail. Thus, in order to keep the system in place, it is important for whites to develop a sense of superiority over non-whites. The organizer identifies this process as one of *internalizing racial oppression*. This occurs when the ideology of race has been internalized by the members of the race-structured society. In the case of whites, the process is referred to as *internalizing racial superiority*.

On the other hand, the process of internalizing racial oppression by non-whites is referred to as *internalizing racial inferiority*. When non-whites internalize inferior and subordinate images of themselves, they become fearful of challenging the institutions which have disempowered them. Having an understanding of the process of disempowerment, the organizer relies on her/his knowledge of people's culture and history to organize them into a self-conscious force and to develop accountable leaders. *The understanding of the process of disempowerment increases the possibility of effective organizing across racial lines. It enhances the chances of equitable working relations by preventing the dominant race from controlling the agenda. Furthermore, it offers greater assurance that everyone, regardless of race, will be accountable to the organizing effort and share in the responsibility in taking risks.*

A fourth assumption which undergirds the ethics of undoing racism is that *institutional gatekeepers are im-*

portant to both the maintenance of oppression and the process of community empowerment. The role of gatekeeper is necessary for institutions to effectively perform their function in maintaining the status quo. In a race-structured society, the maintenance of the status quo is to perpetuate racial inequity. So that, from the institutional point of view, the gatekeeper's function is to maintain the institution's oppressive relationship to the community. By gatekeeper we mean anyone in an institutional/organizational role or position who can grant or deny access to institutional resources or equity. This definition is broad enough to include practically any professional position in any institution. For instance, educators, whether teachers, counselors, or administrators, function as gatekeepers in terms of providing access to a quality educational experience. The social expectations of urban schools in the United States is that they are not on par with suburban schools in offering a quality educational experience. When administrators, counselors, and teachers who work in urban schools conform to society's low expectations and maintain low educational standards, they are carrying out their roles as institutional gatekeepers, in this case, by denying significant segments of the population access to a quality educational experience. Similar examples may be made in any profession. Social workers, lawyers, police officers, judges, doctors, journalists, clergy people, real state agents, insurance agents, people who work for banks and lending institutions as well as foundations, politicians, etc., are all in position to grant or deny access to resources or equitable treatment.

Gatekeepers are, by structural design, accountable to the institutions they work for and not the clients they serve. They function as buffers between their institutions and the community. A buffer is one who protects the institution by intercepting or moderating adverse

23

pressures or influences on it. To allow racial minorities to have the same access to institutional resources as the dominant race would create adverse pressures on institutions which, in a race-structured society, were created by whites to serve the interest of white people. Institutional gatekeepers are therefore important to the maintenance of the status quo because as buffers they protect the institutionalized arrangement which perpetuates the superiority of whites.

Institutionalized gatekeepers are not the only buffers which protect the interest of white institutions. Racial/ethnic immigrant groups may also be used by the system to function as buffers which protect the institutionalized arrangement of white superiority. Upon their entry into the United States, many of these groups become aware of the racial hierarchy with whites occupying the top rung and blacks occupying the bottom. The quest to conform to the racial norms of the United States causes such immigrants to internalize racial stereotypes about blacks. Their internalization of such stereotypes allows them to accept and justify the inequitable racial arrangement. When they establish small businesses in black communities, they often bring with them the racial stereotypes and behavior that foster divisiveness between the groups. It is common for people to identify such inter-group conflict as racism between the two groups. In truth, neither group controls the institutional resources of society. Moreover, as long as one group perceives the other as the enemy, and not the racist system which pits them against each other, the institutions are protected from the adverse pressure of a united struggle for racial equity.

Community organizers and activists may also function in the capacity of a buffer. Whenever such persons refuse to be accountable to the leadership development of their constituents, they are, in essence, protecting the status quo by depriving oppressed people of the skills and hope of gaining access to the institutions which control their lives. When agents of social change such as activists and organizers devalue an accountable relationship with a constituency group, they send the message that equitable institutional change is not the goal. Institutions often view such a person's pressure tactics as an attempt to get a job. When these pressure tactics are successful and the activist is bought off by the system, the constituency group remains leaderless and disempowered. Hence, the pressure of an authentic movement for social change has been effectively abated.

Oftentimes such activists are well-intentioned. Inspired by the motivation to do good, it is not uncommon for persons who are both unfamiliar with the ethics of undoing racism and who lack necessary organizing skills to become passionately involved in social change work. Activists like this tend to believe that because they care about the poor and the disadvantaged, they are qualified to act in the people's behalf. The results of such efforts are generally confusion and distrust. This, of course, leads to the disorganization of the community and the institutions which oppress the people remain unthreatened. Organizers must recognize that caring about people is not enough to heal an oppressed community. Just as one who cares about sick people would not consider performing a medical operation without the proper training, neither should a caring lay person attempt to operate on a community in need of healing. The results are inevitably disastrous.

Another type of unaccountable activist or organizer that functions as a buffer to institutional change is the charismatic leader. Rather than create an accountable organizational structure, the charismatic leader depends on charm or the power of a persuasive personality to get things done. In this case, the constituents have such confidence in the leader's ability to articulate the issues that the group rarely develops the skills to sustain the struggle without the leader's guidance. Usually this type of leader has no desire to be held accountable for her/his actions and will not teach the others how to structure an organization in order to do so. Because the charismatic leader rarely envisions an empowered constituency which can sustain a proactive struggle for institutional access, the people are usually unable to function without the leader and the institutions remain unthreatened.

Hence, institutional gatekeepers, ethnic immigrants, and unaccountable community activists function as important buffers which help to maintain institutionalized racial oppression. But how can such buffers be important to the process of empowerment? The answer to this question lies in the capacity of those in buffer positions to internalize the ethics of undoing racism. Just as the institutional gatekeeper is in position to close the gate of access and opportunity, so too can that same person open the gate by establishing accountable relationships with community-based constituency groups. Such gatekeepers who are employed in banks and lending institutions, for instance, may use the Community Reinvestment Act as a vehicle by which to educate and motivate oppressed people to gain greater access to financial resources. Police officers with undoing racism ethics can drastically reduce the disproportionate arrest rate of African American youth, by working closer with families, religious institutions and community-based organizations to establish and maintain programs of hope in the communities. Corporate gatekeepers with humanistic ethics can develop accountable relationships with constituency groups and volunteer a few hours per week to mentor disempowered youth to help prepare them for future careers as "community-minded" professionals.

In virtually every institution, the role of gatekeeper can be useful to the process of empowering people when the person in the gatekeeping role lives by the ethics of undoing racism. Community organizers and activists, in order not to function as buffers, must deeply value sustaining accountable relationships to their constituencies and actively engage in the process of developing accountable anti-racist leaders.

The fifth assumption which undergirds the ethics of undoing racism is that *social change agents must have a viable working definition of racism in order to successfully attain their organizing goals.* A working definition of racism functions as a guide to attain equity and inclusiveness. Moreover, it increases the likelihood of addressing the concerns of the "minority races." The process of undoing racism means being as humanistic as possible when addressing other issues. For instance, the movement for women's rights only relates to the concerns of white women until it is guided by a viable definition of racism that permits the movement to be inclusive of the concerns of all women. In order to achieve equity in the process of organizing, one's definition of racism must be more than merely an academic one. It must be one which works to guide the organizing effort and achieve noticeable results.

The remainder of this manuscript will articulate the definition and meaning of racism used by the People's Institute for Survival and Beyond. This definition has guided our work and has helped thousands of people throughout the United States gain greater control of their lives as they struggle to attain a more equitable society. In the following pages we will explore our working definition of racism as well as how it manifests itself both in the United States and Japan.

THE DEFINITION AND MEANING OF RACISM

The People's Institute views racism as an equation in which the formula reads RACE PREJUDICE + POWER = RACISM. Since a definition of each of the concepts inherent within the formula is necessary in order to understand the equation, let us begin with the definition of the word "race."

III The Meaning of Race

The word "race" is often confused with the word "culture." The two terms, though, are as different as politics is from nature. Indeed, the word "race" is a political concept whereas "culture", as used here, refers to the ethnic origins of a people. A people's ethnic origins or ethnicity is directly related to a location on the planet from which such people naturally originate. Hence, if a specific ethnic group has its origins on the Asian continent, such a group would have Asian cultural characteristics. The same would be true for Europeans and Africans, Native Americans, *etc.*. Culture, then is a group's natural relationship to humanity. In expressing one's relationship to many cultures, the term "multicultural**ism**" may be used to indicate a positive relationship to humanity. On the other hand, the term "rac**ism**" is used to indicate a negative relationship between one race and the remainder of humanity. People who identify themselves as having humanitarian values do not wish to be associated with racism. This is because, in its rigid classification of human beings, "race" has no other function except the political one of dividing humanity into superior/inferior beings. A muti**cultural**ist seeks equity with many cultures. A **racist** has legitimized superiority over all other races.

By "race" we mean:

A specious classification of human beings created by

Europeans (whites) which assigns human worth and social status using "white" as the model of humanity and the height of human achievement for the purpose of establishing and maintaining privilege and power.

Key to this definition is the word "specious" which means, "seemingly fair but not so." In other words, whites created the concept of "race" to unfairly classify all other races as being inferior. For instance, even though Europeans were the numerical minorities in the world, the 18th century European scholars, George Louis Leclerc Buffon and Johann Friedrich Blumenbach, who were the cofounders of the science of anthropology, created a racial hierarchy using Europeans as the norm and all other peoples as exotic variations of white people. The scientific classifications of humans by race which has since emerged from the work of these European scholars include the following races: Caucasoid, Mongoloid and Negroid. The Caucasoids represent the Caucasian race, a term which comes from the single skull that Blumenbach found in the Caucasian Mountain region of Russia. Similarly, the term Mongoloid comes from skulls collected in the Mongolian area of Asia. Both the Caucasian Mountains and Mongolia are geographic locations on planet earth. But what about the Negroid race? Is there a place called Negro land on the planet from which all Negroes originate? Obviously not, this was the term used by Europeans to dehumanize all African peoples during the time of the European enslavement of Africans. Thus, the specious racial classification of "Negroid" justified the enslavement of African People by whites rather than being a "fair" classification of human beings. Thus, it will be normal to treat Negroes unfairly.

Still another example of how the concept of race is a specious one is the use of the color scheme. The color scheme suggests that the races may be classified according to colors. Based on this scheme the colors of the races are white (Europeans), yellow (Asians), brown (Latinos), red (Native Americans), and black (Africans). The white race is the highest among the races which means it has more human worth and social status than all of the other races. On the other hand, the black race is the lowest among the races.

The reason this is a specious scheme is because the color of a racial group does not necessarily correspond to the color assigned to its race. For example, all Africans are considered members of the black race. So that the white French in North African countries such as Tunisia treat the native Tunisians as inferior to the French. Yet, when native Tunisians, who are a lighter skin tone than sub-Saharan Africans, move from Tunisia to the United States, they may be reclassified as "white" even though they remain Africans and will be treated as "black" by the white French when they return home to Tunisia. Are North Africans members of the white or black race?

A similar analogy can be made with the Japanese. According to the color scheme, the Japanese people are supposed to be members of the yellow race. Yet, when Japanese leave Japan to live in South Africa, their racial classification changes to "white". They become "honorary white" citizens of South Africa because of their economic and technological influence in that country. If the South African government would not grant the Japanese the "honorary white" status and insist that they remain members of a lesser race, the Japanese would simply withdraw all of their economic, electronic and technological resources from South Africa which would seriously hurt the South African economy. Hence the question, are Japanese members of the yellow race or the white race?

The concept of race, then, is a specious concept because it is a political classification of human beings rather than a scientific one. That is to say that it is a particular government or a body of law that is the determining factor in identifying one's race and not necessarily one's genetic or cultural heritage. What is more, one individual person may actually be more than one race depending upon the criteria for racial membership of a particular political jurisdiction. In the United States, for instance, a person's race may change depending upon the particular state of the union that such a person lives in. To clarify this point let us consider how the state of Louisiana defines racial membership. According to Louisiana law one is a member of the black race if such a person possesses 1/32 black blood in their veins. This fraction in itself demonstrates that race is not a scientific classification because according to the science of mathematics, 1/32 is much less than 31/32. When two numbers have the same denominator, the one with the largest numerator is the largest number. If then, a person is 31/32 white and only 1/32 black, such a person should scientifically be white since 31/32 is the larger number. Yet, exactly the opposite is true by Louisiana's law. In some Southern states in the U.S., the criteria for being black is 1/8 black blood. This is significant because the 1/8 black blood line does not go back quite as far as the 1/32 black blood line. This being the case, a person born in Louisiana who is 1/32 black and thus a member of the black race in Louisiana can move to another Southern state in the United States and can become white because of the 1/8 black blood criteria. While this may seem absurd to some people, the fact of the matter is that people who live in the State of Louisiana take the matter of race very seriously. In fact, there are many people who have lived as illegitimate "whites" all of their lives and are terrified at the possiblity of the world discovering that they are in fact legitimately members of

33

the "black" race. Consider the case of Susie Guillory Phipps. Mrs. Phipps had lived as a white person all of her life. In an attempt to get a passport to travel to South America with her white husband, she accidentally discovered that her birth certificate indicated that she was black and not white as she thought she was. Believing this to be a mistake, Mrs. Phipps took her case to court in an effort to legitimize her status as a member of the white race. The court conducted a genealogy of Mrs. Phipps which revealed that in 1760 a white slave master in Mobile, Alabama had sexual relations with one of his African slave women who became the ancestors of Mrs. Phipps. Because Mrs. Phipps was able to trace her black heritage back to 1760, sixteen years before the Declaration of Independence was written which led to American Independence from England, the court found that she was 3/32 black. Since 3/32 is more than 1/32, Mrs. Phipps was legitimately black based on Louisiana's law. The tragedy of this situation is that, had Mrs. Phipps lived in any other state in the United States of America, she would have been legitimately "white" and thus able to go with her husband to South America without being ridiculed by the numerical value of her human worth. Hence, the concept of race is a political concept. Because its criteria for membership is defined by a political body, it is, by its very nature, a specious classification of human beings.

IV The Meaning of Prejudice

The word *prejudice* as used in the equation RACE PREJUDICE + POWER = RACISM may be defined as "*an opinion formed before the facts are known; a preconceived idea, usually one that is unfavorable.*" Based on this definition, anyone can be prejudiced regardless of one's race. To be prejudiced, then, is to possess an attitude or belief which may cause unfavorable or discriminatory actions against others on the basis of the prejudice. When the basis of the prejudice is "race," the unfavorable attitude or action may be attributed to the racial difference. So, when the word "race" is used to qualify the word "prejudice," it means that race prejudice occurs when anyone holds preconceived, unfavorable views towards others on the basis of race. It is important to understand this definition of race prejudice in order to comprehend the difference between race prejudice and racism. While race prejudice is simply the preconceived unfavorable attitude or actions against other races, racism is when such attitudes and actions are supported by the power of the law. What then is the meaning of power as it relates to race prejudice?

V The Meaning of Power

It must be understood from the outset that the word "race," which was created by whites, itself implies the prejudice that the white race is superior to all other races. Power, then, in this context is the ability to organize a society based on race and to make legitimate the superiority of the white race.

By power we mean, "having legitimate access to systems sanctioned by the authority of the state." When a society is structured on the concept of race, the white race will always have more access to the state-sanctioned systems than the "inferior races." This is the very reason why the Japanese receive "honorary white" status in South Africa. It does not matter that they are from a non-European culture. The fact of the matter is that since South Africa is a society structured on race, the white race will have greater access to the institutions which grant fairness in legal treatment, economic opportunities and social status. The Japanese will either have the legitimate access to these institutions or they will leave the country and take their resources elsewhere. Thus, the only way they can legitimately have such access is to become "honorary white." It is because of power that whites can make Japanese "white." This means that when Japanese people have been given the "honor" of being "white" in countries outside of Japan, they comply with the norms that maintain racial oppression. Hence, they contribute to the perpetuation and growth of international racism.

In most instances, though, only Europeans are able to qualify as white. This is because Europeans fled Europe and constructed societies in other parts of the world by forcibly taking others' lands and imposing and legitimizing European cultural institutions on non-European peoples. Because non-Europeans have color pigmentation in their skin and Europeans do not, it was necessary for Europeans to construct "the white race" as the model of humanity in order to justify their right to dominate and rule. Hence, the equation **race prejudice + power = racism** suggests that when one race makes legitimate its racial privileges and its power to dominate and control other races, the phenomenon of racism exists.

But it is not enough to simply state that racism may be understood as an equation. It is also necessary to understand how it is manifested into reality. The manifestations of racism, or the ways in which racism is perpetuated in society, takes several basic forms. It is perpetuated through the normative behavior of individuals, through the policies of institutions, through the invasion of a dominant culture, through the medium of language, and through the martial enforcement of genocidal policies against a subjugated race (militarism). To better understand these forms of racism, let us discuss them in the context of the Chisom Case mentioned above.

ᗢᗡᗡ THE FORMS OF RACISM ᗢᗡᗡ

VI Normative Behavior
of Individuals

Despite the fact that the voting districts in New Orleans, Louisiana, were arranged to discriminate against blacks, white New Orleanians conformed to this arrangement and kept the black New Orleanians politically powerless. In other words, whites would not challenge the discriminatory legal system even though they knew it was unjust to black people. For whites, it is considered normal for them to have more privileges than blacks. For blacks to be equal to whites is considered abnormal by whites. As long as every individual white person in New Orleans accepted as normal the racially discriminatory voting districts which gave whites more political clout than blacks, it was guaranteed that no blacks would ever become a Supreme Court Justice of the State of Louisiana. For white New Orleanians to want a black supreme court justice would be to deviate from white norms. Such people would be considered as deviants and may be subjected to threats and intimidation by the normal whites who wish to maintain the status quo.

In order to maintain the racist political districts it is also necessary for every individual black person to conform to norms which keep them powerless. They are also expected to never develop the political sophistication to legally challenge the state's high court. That is why when blacks such as Ronald Chisom and a host of others successfully challenged it legally, it was forced to change. Hence, the maintenance of racism, which in this case involves the political voting districts, requires that all individuals, both black and white, conform to the normal patterns of behavior that keep the racist system in place.

VII Institutional Racism

The reason the discriminatory voting system lasted as long as it did was because it was institutionalized. To be institutionalized means that it had been systematically structured and made legitimate by whites as the process by which voting would occur. Like all other political institutions in the United States, it was structured by whites to benefit the self-interest of white people. Thus, when white people conform to the policies of the institutions which legitimize white superiority, they get privileges over blacks and all other non-white people. These privileges are sanctioned by the law. So, when whites in New Orleans conformed to the discriminatory voting districts, they were guaranteed by law that they would dominate and monopolize all of the Louisiana State Supreme Court Justice seats.

Every institution in the United States is ultimately controlled by whites: from local governments to the national government, from small banks to the federal reserve system, from small health clinics to the major hospitals, insurance and pharmaceutical companies, *etc.*. Despite the fact that the United States is a multi-cultural society, all of the institutions function to render greater benefits to white people. By never challenging the institutional policies which grant them privileges over non-whites, white people maintain more human worth and social status than non-whites and racism remains in place.

Hence, in white societies, the institutions must function to legitimize and perpetuate white superiority. Without the sanctioning granted by the institutions, individual conformity to white privilege would not be possible. In New Orleans, white voters would not have been able to conform to voting exclusively for white supreme court judges if the whites who controlled the state government of Louisiana had not made legitimate the process of diluting the black vote.

But just how did whites come to control the institutions? Why must white institutions sanction white superiority? And finally, why is there the expectation that each and every white individual must conform to norms of white privilege? To understand the answers to these questions requires an understanding of the concept of "Cultural Racism."

VIII Cultural Racism

Cultural racism occurs when one race invades and subjugates another race and imposes a dominant and oppressive political culture on the subjugated race. By culture we mean the way of life of a people. A people's culture is the life blood of their existence. When people become disconnected from their cultural traditions, customs, religious practices and beliefs, *i.e.* their way of life, they become vulnerable to external manipulation and control.

Just as culture is a people's way of life, political culture is the way of life of a political group. Since the concept of white is not an ethnic concept but a political one, the notion of white culture is a political culture whereby the way of life of white people makes it normal for them to have more human worth and social status than nonwhite people. White culture as a superior political culture has historically been sanctioned by the authority of the state. At all times when the word "white" appeared in state constitutions in the United States or on "Jim Crow" racial segregation signs, it granted white people privileges over nonwhite people. In South Africa the word "white" has the same historical function. Hence, white culture is a political culture which is rooted in the specious concept of race. Moreover, it is sanctioned by the authority of the state and necessarily implies the superiority over nonwhite cultures.

42

In Louisiana, like elsewhere in the Western Hemisphere, whites invaded the land, committed genocide against the Native Americans and legitimized white's right to rule and to impose white cultural values on to the people's lives. The Native Americans' values which kept the air, water, and land pure were replaced by white values. After the whites decimated huge populations of Native Americans with guns and white diseases, they created cultural and political institutions which sanctioned their right to rule and to seriously injure the ecological system in the name of "white progress."

When the Native Americans refused to work for the white people, they forcibly kidnapped Africans and coerced them into slavery. Many Africans escaped enslavement by joining camps of Native Americans and sharing their cultural traditions. Some of the traditions of the Native Americans in the New Orleans, Louisiana area have been kept alive by Africans who shared their culture with the Natives. These "Black Indians," as they are still called today, proudly celebrate the sharing and unity of their cultures as an annual event during the Mardi Gras celebrations.

Once whites successfully killed off the vast majority of Native American cultures in Louisiana, they institutionalized African inferiority and made legitimate their normal patterns of behavior that maintained white superiority. It thus became an expectation that all whites would conform to a cultural system of values, beliefs, traditions and laws which would assure their superiority over the Africans. This is cultural racism, the imposition of a racial political culture upon the lives of another race.

IX Linguistic Racism

Linguistic racism occurs when the language of the dominant race is imposed upon the subjugated race. The dominant race creates words which define itself as the model of humanity and the height of human acheivement. An example of this is the word "European." It so happens that the prefix "eu" means "good" or "well-being." Thus, a *Eu*ropean comes from a "good" race; one whose state-of-being is well. In the context of a race structured society, it would be inconsistent with reality for *Eu*ropeans to be less well off than the indigenous populations and/or the enslaved people of whom they have subjugated.

The dominant race (whites) also creates words which function to dehumanize the subjugated race. Because Europeans are the creators of the concept of race and the architects and beneficiaries of institutional racism, it is the Europeans' words that are imposed upon non-European peoples. The Europeans' creation of the words "Negro," "mulatto," and "creole" are all examples of this.

The word "Negro" emerged in the European languages during the time when many European countries were kidnapping and trading in African slaves. "Negro" was the word they created for all Africans and became the name for their "black cargo." It had its origins with the Latin word "niger" which means black and the Greek word "nekros" which means corpse. A successful shipment of "Negro Slaves" would put a European slave merchant "in the black" in terms of his financial standings. In other words, the kidnapping, the bondage and the selling of "Negroes" was a profitable enterprise for Europeans. Thus in the mind of the Europeans, the "Negro" was not a human being but a commodity to be used for the production of wealth. There existed no word for the African in the European languages that conceptualized the "Negro" as a human. To treat them as human would have been a denial of the European construct of reality. In other words, because there existed no word which associated the Negro with humanity, to treat Black people as human beings would have been considered deviant or pathological behavior based on the reality of Europeans.

The Europeans creation of the word "mulatto" has a similar history. Because whites were considered the "pure breed" and the Negroes were considered by whites to be an "impure breed," the Europeans created the word "mulatto" as the name for the off-spring of a white and Negro sexual union. The Latin root of the word "mulatto" is "mulis" which is the same root for "mule" or the off-spring of a horse (pure breed) and a jackass (impure breed). Thus, from the European perspective, the mulatto was not a pure blooded human being because of the impure "Negro" blood in its veins.

In Louisiana, where the French preceded the English invasion of the Native Americans' land, the French language was the official one until the Louisiana Territory was purchased by the United States in 1803. By then the French had already created their own word for the off-spring of a European and a Negro. The word is "Creole." Used in this manner, the word "Creole" is a person of mixed European and Negro ancestry who speaks a Creole dialect. Hence, the word "Creole" is the French word for "Mulatto." Neither is fully human.

One of the effects of linguistic racism is that the non-European victims who must use these words to define themselves often internalize the values implicit in the words. These words suggest that whites are supposed to have more human worth and social status than non-human Negroes and half-breed Mulattoes and Creoles. When the Negroes, Mulattoes and Creoles internalize this world view, they perceive themselves as being less valuable than whites and conform to their very own oppression. In short, they internalize the oppression of the social meaning of the words. They learn to value "white" above all else. It is not unusual for Mulattoes and Creoles to consider themselves "better than" darker-skinned Black people. For instance, in New Orleans there are Creoles who value white skin to such an extent that they refuse to let their daughters marry another Creole whose skin is darker than a brown paper bag. Thus, when oppressed people internalize the oppression of these words, they become divided amongst themselves. This makes their struggle for equity and justice fragmented and ineffective. Hence, linguistic racism functions to make Black liberation, not just unachievable but unthinkable. It is for this reason that oppressed people must redefine themselves and undo the racism in the language which defines them as inferior beings to whites.

X Militarism as Racism

Militarism is the glorification of the ideals of a professional military class. A culture structured on militarism, *i.e.,* a militaristic society, is one in which military preparedness is of primary importance to the state. The invasion, conquest and reign of the Europeans over non-European peoples of the world requires a militarized state. In the United States, for instance, the whites "won the west" from the American Indians by the ultimate use of force by the U.S. military. Similarly, the slave codes of the American South were readily enforced by state militia. Even when Africans would escape their bondage by running away, whites could be deputized by the state to use force of arms to capture and resubjugate the Black freedom seekers. Indeed, it was the United States military that forcibly acquired the entire Southwestern United States from the Mexican government.

During the Civil Rights Movement in the 1950s and 1960s, racists public officials would mobilize the state militia and the National Guard to prevent non-violent freedom marchers from gaining social equality. When the urban riots erupted in the Black communities in the North during the 1960s, the National Guard, rather than job opportunities, was white America's solution to the poverty and discontent of Blacks. To this very hour, the National Guard strategically surrounds Black communities throughout the United States to quell the first sign of urban unrest.

The very existence of white society depends upon the dehumanization of the subjugated non-European people and the appropriation of their natural resources. Because of this, the institutions of socialization, *i.e.,* the media, the family and the schools, must condition youth to glorify the ideals of the military and devalue the lives of non-Europeans. By watching television children learn that the white cowboys are the good guys and the Indians are the bad guys. They learn that Black people are violent criminals and that Mexicans (Hispanics) are bandits and illegal aliens. They are constantly bombarded with armed-services' commercials which influence them to "BE ALL YOU CAN BE: JOIN THE ARMY." And they come to believe that white men are the super heroes of the world who can fly in the air, bend steel with their bare hands and represent "truth, justice and the American way."

Parents of young boys buy them toy guns, toy hand grenades and camouflage uniforms so that they can live out their childhood fantasies of killing their enemies and dying heroically. Toy male dolls such as "G.I. Joe" provide boys with the appropriate gender role models to defend the interest of white America. War games in the video stores prepare America's youth for both the hand-eye coordination and the insensitivity to perform distance-killing and depersonalized modern warfare.

In the schools, children are programmed to memorize the Pledge of Alligiance to America's flag and to develop historical amnesia as to the truth of white people's genocidal relationship with the rest of humanity. They learn to forget how the newly arrived European immigrants denounced their ethnic identities and acquired the racial identity of white in order to have more human worth and social status than non-whites. They learn to reinterpret historical events so that rather than being murderous invaders, the whites were simply innocent settlers. The guidance counselors in working-class and poor communities help the military recruiters by channeling high school graduates and drop-outs in to the armed services. Once enlisted, these politically naive adolescents are able to prove their manhood by enduring the training that makes them uniformed killers for America.

Even as this process is taking place, the soaring unemployment and poverty in the communities of America's minorities are sustained by the U.S. Government's unwillingness to allocate enough money in the federal budget to create the necessary jobs to improve the quality of life of the poor. Instead, a disproportionate amount of the budget is allocated for military expenditures. This is because in a racist, militaristic society, the stockpiling of sophisticated weapons have more value than the lives of human beings, especially non-white ones. It was precisely this condition that led the late Dr. Martin Luther King, Jr. to declare that, "A nation that continues year after year to spend more money on military defense than on programs of social uplift is approaching spiritual death."

The success of the United States' Government in militarizing the minds of its youth has historically led Black Americans to enlist in the military to take orders from whites to kill the Native Americans. It has led Japanese Americans, whose property was taken from them by the white U.S. Government, to support the white government's efforts to destroy Japan. It has led Black Americans, Native Americans and Japanese Americans to kill the people in South East Asia so that wealthy white Americans can control more of the world's natural and human resources. In recent years the non-white countries throughout Central America as well as Lebonan, Grenada, Libya, Iraq, *etc.* have all experienced the hor-

49

ror of white terror via U.S. foreign policy. It is for these reasons that U.S. militarism may be veiwed as the martial enforcement of genocidal policies against the non-white populations of the world.

Militarism, like the other forms of racism, relates to the Chisom Case. Like other cities throughout the United States, the city from which the Chisom case emerged, New Orleans, Louisiana, is a city that glorifies racist slave masters and military war heroes. A quick glimpse through the New Orleans' telephone directory will reveal the historical depths of how racism and militarism continue to permeate the values of that city. In the telephone directory one will find schools that carry the name of a racist who was a slave master and streets named in the honor of military heroes whose claim to glory was defending a racist state. The John McDonough Schools, for instance, were named after the slave master who owned more slaves than any other masters in the history of the United States. In addition, there are numerous streets named after racists war heroes of the American South such as Andrew Jackson, the Indian killing, slave master General of the U.S. military who became the 7th president of the United States. Another such boulevard is named after Jefferson Davis, the president of the racist Confederacy during the American Civil War. It is no coincidence that, in a city that has enshrined racism and militarism into the very fabric of the values of its society, Black citizens had to sue the state government to get fair representation on the state Supreme Court.

The process of undoing racism is based on understanding the depth of the meaning of racism and how it is manifested in society. It would be incorrect to believe that racism has been undone in New Orleans just because a Black person will be seated on the Louisiana Supreme Court. This represents nothing more than a small part of the total process of undoing racism, the part of influencing social policy. The larger part is the transformation of normative behavior patterns that maintain a racists status quo. For, even if there is policy change, the racist norms and values will eventually prevail and undo the gains of the anti-racist policy. This is precisely what happened during the Reagan adminstration when the civil rights' gains of racial minorities were reversed as whites made legitimate the argument that they were the most discriminated group because their white privilege had been challenged.

Undoing racism is therefore a life-style that must continue throughout one's life span. It must involve accountable anti-racists community organizers of all races who will not stop organizing at the point of policy change but will continue to develop anti-racist community leaders. For instance, it is quite possible that the Black person on the Supreme Court will not be accountable to the Black community who made the position possible. Such a person could easily forget his/her constituency and make decisions, like the white judges, who maintain the racists status quo. It is therefore important that community organizers possess the intelligence and the integrity as well as the values and the vision that will develop conscious local community leaders. These organizers and leaders must educate their communities to elect responsible Black judges and hold them accountable to making decisions of justice once in office.

But even accountable judges will not in themselves undo racism. This will require the weight of a mass movement of social justice, a movement inspired by anti-racists values. For as long as the society is structured on the specious concept of race, racism will be inevitable. This means that white dominance will continue to assert itself within the United States and around the world as the model of humanity for the purpose of maintaining white privilege and power. It is for this reason that the undoing racism philosophy is an international philosophy of social change.

UNDOING RACISM
AND JAPAN

XI Undoing Racism and Japan

Japan provides an excellent example of how the undoing racism philosophy must be applied internationally. The United States government depends on the Japanese to conform to white values and to promote the self-interests of whites in the international community. The U.S. thus uses its military might to, in part, assure Japan's conformity to U.S. interest. After the United States defeated Japan in World War II, it appointed itself policeman of the free world and intervened militarily in Japan. As a result of the U.S. occupation of Japan between 1945-1952, Japan's security system, the Self-Defense Forces (SDF) was developed as a miniature version of America's armed forces. The United States does not permit the SDF to have nuclear weapons; neither is Japan permitted to fight beyond the boarders of Japan. The rules are that Japan can fight only if attacked, and then only on home ground. In essence, Japan's military forces are merely an auxiliary to U.S. global strategy. Its function is to supplement U.S. power in East Asia and protecting Japan is simply a by-product. According to the distinguished Japanese politician, Shintaro Ishihara, this arrangement makes Japan "vulnerable because our defenses were built in accordance with Washington's wishes, not our own priorities."[1]

The vulnerability that Ishihara makes reference to is based on the Japan-U.S. partnership which he believes is structured to foster a "subservient mentality" among the Japanese. Throughout the eleven chapters and epilogue of his controversial book, *THE JAPAN THAT CAN SAY NO,* Shintaro Ishihara admonishes the Japanese to be aware of the race prejudice of whites. The "Japanese should not forget that Caucasians are prejudiced against Orientals," he warned in the second chapter entitled "Racial Prejudice: The Root Cause of Japan-Bashing." In chapter six he points out: "Class-conscious and racist attitudes are deeply entrenched in the Caucasian psyche. No matter how much non-whites object, Westerners will not soon shed their prejudice."[2] Hence, to Ishihara, the Japan-U.S. partnership is hampered by the race prejudice of whites, who as he put it ". . . really think that we are inferior, still unworthy of their admiration and respect."[3]

It was quite perceptive on Shintaro Ishihara's part to question the "subserviant mentality" that whites expect the Japanese to acquire. Indeed, the vast majority of Japanese do not recognize how the agents of socialization in Japan perpetuate white values and function to replace traditional Japanese values with those of the white world. For instance, the family has always been the basic unit of organization in Japanese society. The stability of the family unit is the core of the strength and the perserverence of Japanese traditions. Yet, while still miniscule compared to the total number of families in Japan, there has been a startling increase in the divorce rates over the past decades. If this current trend is allowed to proliferate, it will present a threat to the sacred value and stability of the Japanese family. If the causes of marital divorce are not adequately addressed, this deleterious trend, in generations to come, may eventually undermine the very institution that has made Japan such a cohesive and powerful nation.

It can be reasonably speculated that the increase in

Japanese divorce rates are, to a considerable extent, the result of white influences on Japanese youth. The traditional concept of arranged marriages is gradually being supplanted by the white tradition of romantic love. In that romantic love is an ephemeral emotion based on personal and physical attractiveness, it can not provide the commitment to sustain the family as an endurable social institution. Because of this, such marriages often end in divorce, which constitutes official social recognition that a marriage has failed. Yet, despite the fact that the divorce rate in the United States is believed to be the highest in the world, Japanese youth are so influenced by white American values that there is an increasing tendency, although seemingly imperceptable, for them to denounce their own tradition of arranged marriages as being out-dated.

Although this gradual shift in values is going almost completely unnoticed by most of the Japanese, few can deny the popularity among Japanese youth of American popular culture. The daily bombardment of white values in books, magazines, comics, records, billboards, movies and television serve the function of mentally conditioning the population to accept the explicit and implicit values in these medium. Hence, Japanese youth are subliminally developing a "subserviant mentality" to the white world by embracing the images and the inherent values of white popular culture.

This "subserviant mentality" to the white world is cultivated in the Japanese mind by their acceptance of white values as truth. Such loyal acceptance of the values of whites not only threatens to gradually usurp traditional Japanese values in Japan, but it also prepares the Japanese people to be apologist for white dominance around the world. The maintainance of white dominance over nonwhite people throughout the world requires the acceptance of a worldview which purports that whites are superior to nonwhites. While whites do not expect the Japanese to internationally promote their own inferiority to whites, there does exists the expectation that in the new world order the Japanese will align themselves with whites in justifying the inferiority of others, especially Africans. Since the continent of Africa possesses most of the mineral resources needed for the technological advancements of the 21st century, it is important to the white industrialized countries to influence the Japanese to denigrate Africans rather than to independently ally themselves with African countries. This, in part, explains why in the 1980s U.S. Congressmen demanded that Japan pledge not to help Libya build a chemical plant after they had falsely accused the Japanese of assisting Libya in the production of poison gas. Shintaro Ishihara describes the affair like this:

Today, many Americans overract if Japan has the temerity to act like an independent nation. This happened with the FSX [Fighter Support Experiment]. Using their standard technique of fabricated charges, congressmen attacked the Mitsubishi Group as a way of getting at MHI [Mitsubishi Heavy Industries]. They claimed that Mitsubishi was helping Libya to build a chemical plant to produce poison gas. Later, the allegations were shown to be completely false. Undeterred by truth, these august legislators then demanded that Japan pledge not to help the Libyans build the facility in the future! It was as if a person accused of theft was shown to be innocent, and then the accusers, instead of apologizing, demanded that he promise never to steal again. This is the country that professes to treat Japan as an equal.[4]

In the quest for economic dominance the Japanese pose a potentially formidable threat to the United States' access to Africa's resources. To prevent this threat from becoming a reality it is necessary for the United States to influence the Japanese to perceive all blacks as subhumans who are inferior to Japanese and thus unworthy of their alliance. For instance, when former prime minister of Japan, Nakasone Yasuhiro, and several other Japanese officials made negative remarks about black Americans, the United States government did nothing to correct the derogatory, stereotypic images of blacks for the Japanese public. Moreover, every stereotype that white Americans created to belittle African Americans over the past centuries have been imported to Japan and sold as consumer goods. The images of blacks on Japanese television reinforce the stereotype that black people are dangerous criminals. In short, the white influences in Japanese political and popular culture function to create and perpetuate, in the Japanese mind, the idea that blacks are inferior beings who have no status in the international community.

It is for these reasons that the philosophy of undoing racism must be applied in Japan. As long as the Japanese unquestionably accept white values and images as truth, they will maintain and reproduce their own "subserviant mentality" to whites. Since racism manifests itself in Japan by indoctrinating the Japanese with white values, the Japanese can expect a gradual erosion of traditional Japanese values and a collective prejudice against blacks. Both may result in Japanese vulnerability to white manipulation. Hence, in Japan, undoing racism means challenging the penetration of white values and consciously struggling to stop racism against blacks in Japan. Indeed, the struggle to stop racism against blacks in Japan is a frontal assault on the incursion of the very values that will prevent Japan from being independent in world affairs. As long as the Japanese must seek "honorary white status" instead of being "honorable in their relations" with other nations in the non-European world, they will always be inferior to whites. Therefore, undoing racism in Japan will help liberate the Japanese from white subserviance and the rest of the world from white oppression.

End Notes

<u>Undoing Racism and Japan</u>

1. Shintaro Ishihara, *The Japan That Can Say No* (New York: Simon & Schuster, 1989), p. 72.

2. Ibid., pp. 82-83.

3. Ibid., p. 75.

4. Ibid., p. 77.

CONCLUSION

In conclusion, both the Chisom case and the tendency of Japanese citizens to conform to white values are urgent examples of why the undoing racism philosophy must be put into effective practice by educators, activists, and community organizers. The victory of the Chisom case made it possible for the state of Louisiana to elect its first African American member to the Supreme Court. Moreover, this case has resulted in numerous African American trial and appellate judges being elected in Louisiana and throughout the south. Despite such equitable gains, there are efforts underway in both the Louisiana courts and the federal Supreme Court to invalidate the victories of the Chisom case. In an unpublished document entitled "Institutional Racism in the Electoral Process," Mr. William Quigley, the plaintiff's attorney in the Chisom case, provides a brilliant summation of the case and the related pending court challenges. Mr. Quigley's summary begins with the filing of the Chisom case in 1986. He then provides a discussion of the efforts to eliminate Black majority districts. He ends with a plea to the people in the state of Louisiana to continue the demand for equal voting opportunities in the courts.

According to Quigley, in 1986, Ron Chisom and other black registered voters in Louisiana filed a federal voting rights class action suit against the Governor of Louisiana. Ron Chisom and his lawyers asked that the Louisiana Supreme Court be reapportioned to allow black voters, who are a majority in the City of New Orleans, an opportunity to elect a candidate of their choice. In the entire history of the state, despite the fact that the state is 30% black, no person of color had ever been elected to the Louisiana Supreme Court.

The Suit was based on the federal Voting Rights Act. The Voting Rights Act was passed by Congress in 1965 as a result of the civil rights struggle. This law prohibits denial of the right to vote on the basis of race or any violation of equal opportunity in any part of the electoral process. The suit was brought by civil rights lawyers in Louisiana and lawyers with the NAACP Legal Defense and Educational Fund Inc., in New York. Among the lawyers on the case was Lani Guinier from the NAACP and Bill Quigley from New Orleans.

In Challenging voting discrimination by the State of Louisiana, Ron Chisom joined a long line of distinguished civil rights advocates. For example, Barbara Major took the lead in a federal class action called *Major versus Treen* that ultimately created Louisiana's first black majority Congressional District. As a result of that case William Jefferson was elected the first African American congressional representative from Louisiana in one hundred years. Guinier and Quigley also represented Barbara Major.

The State of Louisiana objected to the Chisom suit saying that the Voting Rights Act had never been applied to elections for judges. At first, the State won. The Chisom case was thrown out of court in 1987 by the trial judge. But the Chisom case was appealed to the U.S. Supreme Court. On June 20, 1991 a 6-3 majority of the Supreme Court agreed with Ron Chisom and decided that the Voting Rights Act did apply to elections for judges. The historic case, called *Chisom v Roemer,* can be found at 111 S. Ct. 2354. The case has been quoted more than one hundred times in other voting rights cases in the years since the decision.

As a result of the Chisom decision, the Louisiana Supreme Court was reapportioned to create a black majority district and Louisiana elected the first African American member of the Louisiana Supreme Court. Other courts around the South were also reapportioned as a result of this case and numerous African American trial and appellate judges were elected in Louisiana and other states.

However, since the decision in Chisom and others in the early 1990s, the Supreme Court has dramatically reversed many of the gains brought about by the Voting Rights Act. A wave of conservative federal judges decided that creating black majority voting districts to allow black voters to elect candidates of their choice are efforts to segregate voters and therefore unconstitutional. They see no such problem with most white majority districts.

The U.S. Supreme Court in a 1993 North Carolina case called *Shaw v Reno* changed voting rights law and made it much more difficult to create districts where black voters could have an opportunity to choose elected officials of their choice. That decision was 5 to 4. The three justices who dissented in the Chisom case (Kennedy, Rehnquist and Scalia) were joined by two other justices, Sandra Day O'Connor, and the newly appointed Justice Clarence Thomas. Together, they reversed decades of voting rights law.

Since that decision, state after state has seen efforts by white voters to dissolve black majority districts and substitute white majority districts. For example, in Louisiana a second black majority congressional district was created by the state legislature in the early 1990s. A federal court ruled that the district discriminated against white voters and redrew the boundaries to create a white majority district.

There are also efforts underway in Louisiana to undo the gains brought by the Chisom case. A white lawyer from a suburb of New Orleans has challenged the creation of the black majority district for the Supreme Court of Louisiana. The case has already been in two federal courts and three Louisiana state courts. It seeks to invalidate the Chisom victory by saying it is racially discriminatory to allow one of the seven Louisiana Supreme Court Districts to have a black majority.

There are also pending court challenges to other black judicial districts on the trial and appeal level in Louisiana. Similar actions to eliminate black majority districts are occurring in Georgia, North Carolina, and other southern states.

The civil rights struggle in the area of voting rights is now on the defensive in the courts. No progress in equal voting opportunity in the courts will occur as long as the U.S. Supreme Court continues to call black majority districts but not white majority districts segregation. The fight in the court right now is not for progress, it is for survival. Progress in voting rights was not created mainly in the courts. Though there were some very important progressive court decisions, progress was initiated by the legislature in response to the demands of the people.

For voting rights to survive, there will have to be changes in the courts, but more importantly, the voices of the people must be raised again and must be heard again. Community organizers must be equipped with an effective process of implementing the undoing racism philosophy if equal voting opportunities will ever be achieved.

JAPAN AND THE CONTINUED STRUGGLE

The tragedy of Japanese citizens conforming to white values provides still another example as to why the undoing racism philosophy must be put into effective practice. The marketing of sambo consumer goods in Japan is at least a multi-million dollar enterprise. Because of the small number of people of African descent in Japan, the prevalent availability of derogatory sambo consumer goods allow Japanese citizens to develop negative stereotypes about black people.

In 1988 a Japanese family in Osaka, Japan, created an organization called The Association To Stop Racism Against Blacks (ASRAB). The purpose of ASRAB is to stop the manufacturing and publishing of Sambo goods in Japan. By using effective strategies and tactics, the ASRAB organization has stopped the production of several black stereotypic consumer products. However, ASRAB's successes have been minimal compared to the vast quantity of sambo consumer goods which continue to be marketed throughout the island country. The publishing companies which publish comic books have been particularly resistant to the ASRAB's movement to rid Japan of racist goods and comics. The resistance by the publishing companies may be attributed to at least three factors. First, the publication of such comics are very profitable. Second, the creator of these comics, Tezuka Osamu, is regarded by the Japanese as the God of Comics. This tends to sanction the idea that the demeaning images of blacks in these comics are worthy of continued publication. A third factor is the lack of international pressure exerted against the publishing companies. As long as citizens throughout the world make no effort to pressure their government and business leaders to force the Japanese to discontinue publishing such racist comics, there can be no expectation that this insidious expression of racist propaganda will come to a stop.

To make matters worse, two new versions of the book *Little Black Sambo* are being resurrected by American authors who are respected figures in children's literature. One of the new versions which is entitled *Sam and the Tigers* is written and illustrated by African Americans. Julius Lester and Jerry Pinkney, have reconfigured the original book by substituting the minstrel-like black characters with a more specific African American slant. The other resurrected version is entitled *The Story of Little Babaji.* Its illustrator is a white man named Fred Marcellino who argues that "the original is a little master piece" whose "good qualities really outweigh its racist elements." Marcellino's approach is to leave the original's simple text as it was and merely replace the character's names with Indian ones with new illustrations. Lester and Pinkney's new version is published by Dial while Marcellino's is published by Harper Collins who, incidentally, continues to sell 20,000 copies a year of the original. In their attempt to resuscitate the original children's classic, which became practically an icon during the Jim Crow era, the question facing the two publishers is: can a renamed and redrawn version of a racially offensive classic be rehabilitated?[1]

Japanese publishers are unconcerned about resuscitating the image of sambo. To them, the mere fact that Americans, especially Black Americans, have repub-

lished a sambo book for children reinforces their ratio-
nale for the continued use of derogatory black stereotypes in their comics. Despite the fact that the Americans are attempting to resuscitate an image which they
view as having racist elements, the Japanese publishers reason that "if Americans see nothing wrong with
publishing sambo books, then why should we?" This is
the reason why there must be a commitment to an international movement to undo racism in Japan and the
world.

End Notes

[1]Belinda Luscombe, "Same Story, New Attitude: Two
Publishers Resuscitate A Children's 'Classic'" *Time*
(September 9, 1996).

References

Davis, James. *Who Is Black.* The Pennsylvania State University Press, 1991.

Franklin, John H. *From Slavery to Freedom,* 7th edition. McGraw-Hill, 1994.

Gossett, Thomas F. *Race.* Schocken Books, 1963.

Higginbotham, A. Leon, Jr. *In the Matter of Color.* Oxford, 1980.

Ishihara, Shintaro. *The Japan That Can Say No.* New York: Simon & Schuster, 1989.

Karenga, Maulana. *Introduction to Black Studies.* Sankore, 1989.

Montagu, Ashley. *Man's Most Dangerous Myth: The Fallacy of Race,* 5th edition. New York: Oxford Press, 1974.

Takaki, Ronald. *Iron Cages.* Oxford, 1990.

_____. *Strangers from Another Land.* Penguin, 1989.

Time Magazine (September 9, 1996):

Selected Bibliography

Abernathy, Ralph D. *And the Walls Come Trumbling Down.* Harper & Row, 1989.

Albert, Michael, and Associates. *Liberating Theory.* South End Press, 1986.

Allport, Gordon W. *The Nature of Prejudice.* Doubleday, 1958.

Alperovitz, Gar, and Faux, Jeff. *Rebulding America.* Pantheon, 1986.

Ashmore, Harry S. *Hearts and Minds.* Seven Locks Press, 1988.

Baldwin, James. *The Evidence of Things Not Seen.* Hold, Rinehart and Winston, 1985.

Banks, James A. *An Introduction to Multicultural Education.* Allyn and Bacon, 1994.

Barndt, Joseph. *Dismantling Racism: The Continuing Challenge to White America.* Philadelphia, PA: Augsburg Press, 1990.

Barone, Michael. *Our Country.* The Free Press, 1990.

Barry, Tom, and Preusch, Deb. *The Central America Fact Book.* Grove, 1986.

Bennett, Leone, Jr. *Before the Mayflower.* Johnson Publishing, 1982.

Boskin, Joseph. *Sambo.* Oxford University Press, 1986.

Brown, Dee. *Bury My Heart at Wounded Knee.* Bantam, 1972.

Brueggemann, Walter. *The Land.* Fortress Press, 1977.

Caldwell, Gilbert H. *Race, Racism and Reconciliation.* Simon Printing, 1989.

Campbell, Christopher P. *Race, Myth and the News.* Sage, 1995.

Campbell, Will D. *Forty Acres and a Goat.* Peachtree, 1986.

Carson, Clayborne. *In Struggle.* Harvard College, 1981.

Cash, W.J. *The Mind of the South.* Vintage, 1960.

Chruchill, Ward, and Wanderwall, Tim. *Agents of Repression.* South End, 1990.

Cleage, Albert B., Jr. *The Black Messiah.* Sheed and Ward, 1968.

Coalition on Human Needs. *How the Poor Would Remedy Poverty.* Coalition.

Cogswell, James A. *No Place Left Called Home.* Friendship Press, 1983.

Comer, James P., M.D. *Maggie's American Dream.* Plume, 1988.

Cone, James H. *God of the Oppressed.* Saabury, 1975.

Cox, Harvey, *Religion in the Secular City.* Simon and Schuster, 1984.

Cross, Theodore. *The Black Power Imperative.* Faulkner, 1987.

Daniels and Kitano. *American Racism: Exploration of the Nature of Prejudice.* Prentiss-Hall, 1974.

Dates, Jannette L., and Balow, William. *Split Image.* Howard University Press, 1990.

Davis, Angela. *Women, Culture, & Politics.* Random House, 1989.

_____. *Angela Davis: An Autobiography.* International, 1988.

_____. *Women, Race & Class.* Random House, 1981.

Dees, Morris. *A Season for Justice.* New York: Scribner's & Son, 1991.

Degler, Carl N. *The Other South.* Northeastern University Press, 1982.

_____. *Out of Our Past.* Harper, 1985.

Dennis, Peggy. *The Autobiography of an American Communist.* Lawrence Hill, 1977.

Douglas, Frederick. *Life and Times of . . . .* Collier, 1962.

DuBois, W.E.B. *The Souls of Black Folk.* Signet, 1982.

Dunbar, Anthony P. *Against the Grain.* University of Virginia, 1981.

Edsall and Edsall. *Chain Reaction: The Impact of Race, Rights, and Taxes on American Politics.* New York: Norton, 1991.

Ezorsky, Gertrude. *Racism and Justice: The Case for Affirmative Action.* Cornell, 1991.

Hunter, James D. *Culture Wars: The Struggle to Define America.* Basic Books, 1991.

Hutchinson, Earl Ofari. *The Mugging of Black America.* Chicago: African American Images, 1990.

Ehle, John. *Trail of Tears.* Anchor, 1988.

Ellwood, David T. *Divide and Conquer.* Ford Foundation, 1987.

Evans, Alice F.; Evans, Robert A.; and Kennedy, William B. *Pedagogies for the Non-Poor.* Orbis, 1987.

Evans, Sara M. *Born for Liberty.* Free Press, 1989.

Felder, Cain H. *Troubling Biblical Waters.* Orbis, 1989.

Fischer, Claude S. *The Urban Experience.* Harcourt, Brace, Jovanovich, 1984.

Flexner, Eleanor. *Century of Struggle.* Antheneum, 1974.

Foreman, Grant. *Indian Removal.* University of Oklahoma Press, 1989.

Fraser, Steven. *Labor Will Rule.* Free Press, 1991.

Frankfort, Ellen. *Kathy Boudin and the Dance of Death.* Stein and Day, 1984.

Franklin, John H. *From Slavery to Freedom,* 7th edition. McGraw-Hill, 1994.

Frederickson, George M. *White Supremacy.* Oxford, 1969.

Friedman, Thomas L. *From Beirut to Jerusalem.* Anchor, 1990.

Freire, Paulo. *Pedagogy of the Oppressed.* Heider and Heider, 1970.

Fussell, Paul. *Class.* Ballantine, 1983.

Garrison, Jim. *On the Trail of the Assassins.* Sheidan Square, 1988.

Gates, Henry L., Jr. *"Race," Writing, and Difference.*

University of Chicago Press, 1987.

Gaylin, Willard, and Associates. *Doing Good.* Pantheon, 1976.

Giddings, Paula. *When and Where I Enter: The Impact of Black Women on Race and Sex in America.* Bantam Books, 1984.

Gitlin, Todd. *The Sixties.* Bantam, 1989.

Glick, Brian. *War at Home.* South End Press, 1989.

Goldberg, Robert A. *Grassroots Resistance.* Wadsworth, 1991.

Gossett, Thomas F. *Race.* Schocken Books, 1963.

Greider, William. *Secrets of the Temple.* Touchstone, 1987.

Grier, William H., and Cobbs, Price M. *Black Rage.* Bantam, 1968.

Guevara, Che. *The Diary of Che Guebara.* Bantam, 1968.

Gutierrez, Gustavo. *The Power of the Poor in History.* Orbis, 1983.

Hale-Benson, Janice E. *Black Children: Their Roots, Culture, and Learning Styles.* The Johns Hopkins University Press, 1986.

Hall, Mitchell K. *Because of Their Faith.* Columbia,

1990.

Halstead, Fred. *Out Now.* Monad Press, 1978.

Handlin, Oscar. *Race and Nationality in American Life.* Doubleday, 1957.

Harding, Vincent. *There Is a River: Black Struggle for Freedom in America.* Harcourt Brace Jovanovich, Publishers, 1992.

_____. *Hope and History.* Orbis, 1990.

Hawke, David F. *Nuts and Bolts of the Past.* Harper and Row, 1988.

Higginbotham, A. Leon, Jr. *Shades of Freedom: Racial Politics and Presumptions of the American Legal Process.* Oxford University Press, 1996.

_____. *In the Matter of Color.* Oxford, 1980.

Fill, Melvyn A. *Hannah Arendt.* St. Martin's, 1979.

hooks, bell. *Black Looks: Race and Representation.* South End Press, 1992.

_____. *Talking Back.* South End Press, 1989.

_____. *Ain't I A Woman: Black Women and Feminism.* South End Press, 1981.   .

Horwitt, Sanford D. *Let Them Call Me Rebel.* Knopf, 1989.

Huggins, Nathan I. *Black Odessey.* Vintage, 1977.

Jackson, George L. *Blood in My Eye.* Black Classic Press, 1990.

Jhally, Sut, and Lewis, Justin. *Enlightened Racism.* Westview Press, 1992.

Johson, Paul. *Modern Times.* Harper and Row, 1983.

Jones, James H. *Bad Blood.* Free Press, 1982.

Karenga, Maulana. *Introduction to Black Studies.* Sankore, 1989.

Katznelson, Ira. *City Trenches.* Pantheon, 1981.

Kelley, Robin, D.G. *Hammer and Hoe.* Chapel Hill.

King, Martin L., Jr. *Where Do We Go from Here.* Harper and Row, 1967.

Kinoy, Arthur. *Rights on Trial.* Harvard, 1983.

Kluger, Richard. *Simple Justice.* Vintage, 1977.

Knowles, Louis L., and Prewitt, Kenneth. *Insitutional Racism in America.* Spectrum, 1969.

Kochman, Thomas. *Black and White Styles in Conflict.* The University of Chicago Press, 1981.

Koning, Hans. *Columbus: His Enterpreise.* Monthly Review, 1976.

Lapham, Lewis H. *Money and Class in America.* Weidenfeld, 1988.

Lenski, Gerhard E. *Power and Privilege.* Chapel Hill, 1984.

Lerner, Michael. *Surplus Powerlessness.* ILMH, 1986.

Linquist, Jack. *Increasing the Impact.* W.K. Kellogg Foundation.

Marty, Martin E. *Prigrims in Their Own Land.* Penguin, 1986.

Maginnis, John. *The Last Hayrides.* Gris Gris, 1985.

Mayfield, Chris. *Growing Up Southern.* Pantheon, 1979.

McElvaney, Williams K. *Good News Is . . . .* Orbis, 1980.

Miles, Robert. *Racism.* Routledge, 1989.

Miller, Arthur. *Timebends.* Grove Press, 1987.

Miler, Marc S. *Working Lives.* Pantheon, 1978.

Mintz, Steven, and Kellogg, Susan. *Domestic Revolutions.* Free Press, 1988.

Moltmann, Jurgen. *The Power of the Powerless.* Harper and Row, 1982.

Montagu, Ashley. *Man's Most Dangerous Myth: The Fallacy of Race,* 5th edition. New York: Oxford Press, 1974.

Montejano, David. *Anglos and Mexicans.* University of Texas Press, 1987.

Moore, Robert B. *Racism in the English Language.* CIBC, 1986.

Morris, Aldon D. *The Origins of the Civil Rights Movement.* Free Press, 1984.

Morrison, Toni. *Race-ing Justice, En-gendering Power.* Pantheon, 1992.

Mosse, George L. *Toward the Final Solution.* University of Wisconsin, 1985.

National Council of Churches. *Can't Jail the Sprit.* NCC, 1988.

National Research Council. *A Common Destiny.* National Academy, 1989.

Nelson, Jack A. *Hunger for Justice.* Orbis, 1980.

Neibuhr, Reinhold. *The Irony of American History.* Scribner, 1962.

O'Malley, Padraig. *Biting at the Grave.* Beacon, 1990.

O'Reilly, Kenneth. *Racial Matters.* Free Press, 1989.

Peoples, James, and Bailey, Garrick. *Humanity.*

West, 1988.

Pierce, Gregory F. *Activism That Makes Sense.* Paulist, 1984.

Piven, Frances F., and Cloward, Richard A. *Poor People's Movements.* Vintage, 1979.

Ridgeway, James. *Blood in the Face.* Thunder's Mouth, 1990.

Rothenberg, Paula S. *Racism and Sexism.* St. Martin's, 1988.

Salvatore, Nick. *Eugene V. Debs.* University of Illinois, 1982.

Schaef, Anne W. *When Society Becomes an Addict.* Harper and Row, 1987.

Schneiter, Paul H., and Nelson, Donald T. *The Thirteen Most Common Fund-Raising Mistakes.* Taft.

Schmookler, Andrew B. *Out of Weakness.* Bantam, 1968.

Sheerin, Mira. *How to Raise Top Dollars from Special Events.* PSMC, 1984.

Silver, James W. *Mississippi: The Closed Society.* Harvest, 1966.

Sklar, Holly. *Washington's War on Nicaragua.* South End, 1988.

Sloan, Irving J. *The Blacks in America.* Oceana, 1977.

Smead, Howard. *Blood Justice.* Oxford, 1986.

Smith, Lillian. *Killers of the Dream.* Norton, 1949.

Sparks, Allister. *The Mind of South Africa.* Knopt, 1990.

Sperber, A.M. *Edward R. Murrow: His Life and Times.* Bantam, 1986.

Sperry, Willard L. *Religion in America.* Beacon, 1963.

Stallard, Karin, and Associates. *Poverty in the American Dream.* South End Press, 1963.

Steel, Ronald. *Walter Lippman . . . .* Vintage, 1980.

Steinberg, Stephen. *The Ethnic Myth: Race, Ethnicity, and Class in America.* Boston: Beacon Press, 1991.

Stone, Clarence N. *Ragime Politics in Atlanta.* Kansas, 1989.

Sugarman, Jule M. *A Citizen's Guide to Changes . . . .* HSIC, 1981.

Synnestvedt, Sig. *The White Response to Black Emancipation.* New York: The Macmillan Company, 1972.

Takaki, Ronald. *Iron Cages.* Oxford, 1990.

_____. *Strangers from Another Land.* Penguin, 1989.

Tawney, R.H. *Religion and the Rise of Capitalism.* Peter Smith, 1962.

Terry, Robert W. *For Whites Only.* Berdmans.

Tonna, Benjamin. *Gospel for the Cities.* Orbis, 1976.

Toynbee, Arnold J. *A Study of History.* Oxford, 1947.

Ventura, Michael. *Shadow Dancing in the USA.* Tarcher, 1985.

Weatherby, W.J. *James Baldwin.* Dell, 1989.

Webb, Walter P. *The Great Plains.* Universal, 1931.

Wheaton, Elizabeth. *Code Name Greenkill.* Georgia, 1987.

Whitefield, Stephen J. *A Death in the Delta.* Free Press, 1988.

Williams, Eric. *From Columbus to Castro.* Vintage, 1984.

Whyte and Whyte. *Making Mondragon.* ILR, 1988.

Wolf, Eric R. *Europe and the People Without History.* California, 1982.

Woodward. C. Vann. *The Strange Career of Jim Crow.* Oxford, 1966.

Wright, Gwendolyn. *Building the Dream*. Pantheon, 1981.

X, Malcolm. *The Autobiography of Malcolm X*. Grove, 1966.

Zinn, Howard. *A People's History of the U.S.*. Harper and Row, 1980.

APPENDIX A
THE UNDOING RACISM WORKSHOP

IN BRIEF. . .

The Undoing Racism Workshop is an intensive two and a half day workshop designed to educate, challenge, and empower people to "undo" the racist structures that hinder effective social change. The training is based on the premise that racism has been consciously and systematically erected and that it can be "undone" if people understand where it comes from, how it functions, and why it is perpetuated.

This workshop is offered by **The People's Institute for Survival and Beyond**, a national multiracial antiracist collective of veteran organizers and educators dedicated to building an effective movement for social change. The People's Institute was founded in 1980, has trained thousands of people in hundreds of communities throughout the United States, and is recognized nationally for the quality of its trainings.

10 REASONS WHY YOUR ORGANIZATION SHOULD HOST AN UNDOING RACISM WORKSHOP

1. To learn how to work more effectively and justly in today's diverse community.

2. To understand what racism is and how it is maintained.

3. To challenge old assumptions about how your

work is (or is not) affected by racism.

4. To develop an accurate analysis of the social concerns you may be trying to address.

5. To reassess the actual "results" of your work.

6. To examine internal issues of control, accountability, and bias.

7. To identify and begin to "undo" racist planning, policies, programs, and procedures.

8. To gain energy and insight for taking new risks and trying new strategies.

9. To help reduce racially motivated scapegoating, hatred, and violence.

10. To open doors for building effective multiracial coalitions.

WHO IS THIS WORKSHOP FOR?

* **Community Organizations**, neighborhood associations, organizations that work for welfare rights, tenant rights, and labor rights. . .

* **Religious Institutions**, congregations, communities, clergy, lay leaders. . .

* **Cultural Institutions**, artists, program directors, administrators. . .

* **Activist Organizations**, civil rights workers, peace and justice workers. . .

* **Social Service Agencies**, social workers, health care providers, administrators. . .

* **Schools**, educators, administrators, students, parents. . .

* **Businesses**, executives, managers, employees . . .

* **Government Agencies**, boards, elected officials . . .

* **Foundations**, philanthropists, corporate funders . . .

* **And Others**. . .

THE UNDOING RACISM WORKSHOP IS. . .
Analyzing Power
Effective organizing requires accurate analysis. We do not just analyze the victims of racism — rather, we analyze the systems that keep racism in place. We examine why people are poor, how institutions and organizations perpetuate the imbalance of power, and who is responsible for maintaining the status quo.

Defining Racism
If we want to undo racism, we must be able to recognize it. Hence, we take seriously the task of defining racism and related terms. Organizers and educators who intend to build effective coalitions need to be very clear about what racism is and what it is not in order to avoid serious strategic and tactical errors.

Understanding the Manifestations of Racism
Racism operates in more than just individual and institutional settings. We examine the dynamics of cultural racism, linguistic racism, and militarism as applied racism.

Learning from History
We take seriously the truth that if we do not learn from history, we are condemned to repeat its mistakes. Racism has distorted, suppressed, and denied not only the history of peoples of color, but the history of white people as well. A correct knowledge of history is a necessary organizing tool as well as a source of personal and collective empowerment.

Sharing Culture
One of the most effective methods of oppression is to deny a people its history and culture. Our training process strongly emphasizes "cultural sharing" as a critical community organizing tool. In the workshop, participants have the opportunity to share aspects of their

culture through story, song, dance, art, poetry, and ritual.

Organizing to "Undo" Racism

How can communities achieve concrete results in dismantling the structures of racism? We examine the principles of effective organizing, the process of community empowerment, the techniques of effective strategizing, and the internal dynamics of leadership development.

TOPICS WE INVESTIGATE ARE. . .

* How racism occurs in everyday life.

* How well-intentioned individuals and institutions unwittingly maintain racist policies, biases, systems, and benefits.

* The origins of racism and its development in the United States.

* The history of the concept of "race."

* The benefits and privileges of being white in a racist society.

* The reality of people of color who have risen to positions of authority in the United States.

* How internalized oppression helps maintain racism.

* The dynamics of granting and withholding resources.

TERMS WE DEFINE ARE. . .

* Racism
* Prejudice
* Bigotry
* White Supremacy
* Race
* Power
* Multi-Racial
* Anti-Racist
* Internalized Racist Oppression
* Gatekeeping
* Organizing
* Mobilizing

* Accountability
* The Effective Organizer

QUESTIONS WE STRUGGLE WITH ARE. . .
* Who benefits from racism?
* Who is used by racism?
* Who are the people and organizations that keep racist structures in place?
* What does the term "white" mean, and where does it come from?
* What is the difference between an organization that is "multi-racial" and an organization that is "anti-racist?"
* How can organizers and service providers be held accountable to the communities they work in?
* What enables individuals and communities to get a sense of their own power?
* How can we move from addressing the symptoms of racism to dismantling the causes of racism?

TECHNIQUES WE EMPLOY ARE. . .
* Cultural Sharing
* Role Plays
* Brainstorming
* Formal Presentations
* Focused Discussions
* Illuminating Exercises
* Problem Solving
* Learning from Each Other's Experiences

Our trainers are experienced group facilitators who are skilled in keeping the workshop focused, pertinent, and engaging.

THE UNDOING RACISM WORKSHOP IS NOT. . .
A Quick Fix

Participants should not expect a "handy formula" or a "quick fix" for abolishing racism in their communities.

Racism is a complex relationship that cannot be undone in ten easy steps.

A Sensitivity Session

We recognize that any honest in-depth discussion of racism will uncover feelings of pain, anger, depression, *etc.* However, the purpose of this workshop is not to conduct a sensitivity or therapy session. We suggest that participants plan to work with such feelings in a separate setting.

A Guilt Trip

Racism workshops in previous decades often focused on "white guilt." Laying guilt trips on people is not a part of our training process.

A Sexism/Classism Workshop

Sexism, classism, and other "isms" are significant issues. However, we assert that racism is the single most critical barrier to building a broad-based movement for social change. Hence, while we attempt to show how these other issues interrelate, we only do so in the context of racism.

A Training in Reducing Individual Acts of Prejudice

Some racism workshops focus on the personal aspects of racism, for example: fostering racial sensitivity, dealing with racist jokes, using appropriate terminology, reducing prejudice on the job, *etc.* While the Undoing Racism Workshop may assist people in addressing these issues, our emphasis is on the dynamics and structure of institutional racism and how communities can organize effectively to undo this system.

A Lecture

The Undoing Racism Workshop is a **work**-shop. Participants will struggle, share, discuss, question, and analyze. No one is permitted to "just listen" because racism cannot be undone by just listening.

THE TRAINING COMMITMENT

At the beginning of each Undoing Racism Workshop, participants commit themselves to some basic guidelines:

*   Staying for the entire time of the workshop — not skipping certain parts or leaving the process early.

*   Participating actively in the work to be done.

*   Listening to one another.

*   Respecting one another.

*   Asking the awkward questions and raising the sensitive concerns.

*   Struggling together, even when the work is difficult.

*   Staying focused on racism, even though many other significant issues are intimately related.

* Avoiding the impulse to search for a "quick fix" to racism.

ADVANCED TRAINING

Individuals who have completed an Undoing Racism Workshop conducted by The People's Institute are eligible to participate in the Institute's Advanced National Training. This five-day event is held annually in the New Orleans area and provides ongoing training for individuals committed to the work of undoing racism.

Organizations that have completed an Undoing Racism Workshop may continue their efforts by participating in a follow-up program with The People's Institute.

FREQUENT QUESTIONS

Q: How long is an Undoing Racism Workshop?

A: A basic workshop requires two and a half days.

Q: How many people may attend the workshop?

A: Between 10 and 40.

Q: Where are the workshops held?

A: Typically, an organization will host a workshop at

a site of its own choosing. Occasionally, The People's Institute also holds open workshops in the New Orleans area.

Q: How much does a workshop cost?

A: The basic fee for hosting a workshop is negotiable and includes the services of 2 or 3 trainers. We can assist groups in figuring out how to make the workshop financially possible.

Q: Is the workshop for whites only?

A: No. Our extensive experience in working for social change has taught us that everyone in a racist society is affected by racism. In order for participants to understand accurately certain things about racism, we always strive to do workshops in racially mixed settings.

Q: How can I arrange to host a workshop?

A: Contact The People's Institute for our brochure on how to set up an Undoing Racism Workshop.

FOR MORE INFORMATION. . .

About The People's Institute, our trainers, or setting-up an Undoing Racism Workshop, please contact:

The People's Institute for Survival and Beyond
1444 North Johnson Street
New Orleans, LA 70116
(504) 944-2354

APPENDIX B
HOW TO SET-UP AN
UNDOING RACISM WORKSHOP

STEP 1 — READ OUR BROCHURES

A careful reading of our introductory brochures will answer many questions about The People's Institute, the Undoing Racism Workshop, and our trainers. Please contact the Institute if you do not have this basic information.

STEP 2 — CLARIFY YOUR NEEDS

Before hosting an Undoing Racism Workshop, it is important for both you and The People's Institute to be clear about what your needs are. Please consider the following questions:

* Why does your organization or community need to have an Undoing Racism Workshop?

* What goals do you hope to achieve by hosting this workshop?

* Are there specific concerns that you hope this workshop will address?

* Is there some particular incident, event, or pressure that is causing your organization or community to consider hosting an Undoing Racism Workshop at this time?

STEP 3 — CLARIFY YOUR CONSTITUENCY

* Who is this Undoing Racism Workshop for?
* Would this workshop be an **in house** training, specifically intended for members of your organization? If so, will participants be invited, urged, or required to attend?
* Would this workshop be a **cooperative** effort, involving two or more organizations, communities, agencies, *etc.*? If so, what specific groups will be working together?
* Would this workshop be **open** to individuals in the local community? If so, what segments of the community will you work to have represented?
* Do you expect that this workshop will be racially mixed? If not, how will you ensure some diversity? Whenever possible, Undoing Racism Workshops are done in racially mixed settings. Exceptions are made only in certain circumstances and with prior agreement by the trainers.

STEP 4 — CALL THE PEOPLE'S INSTITUTE

Once you have read through our brochures and have given some thought to the questions above, please give us a call. We will be happy to answer your questions about the People's Institute and the Undoing Racism Workshop.

If you are interested in pursuing the possibility of hosting a workshop, we would also like to talk with you about your particular needs, your constituency, and some of the details noted below.

STEP 5 — CONSIDER A
PRELIMINARY CONSULTATION

The People's Institute is committed to providing undoing racism training with adequate preparation and follow-up in the local community. We do not see the undoing racism process beginning or ending with simply a workshop.

93

We encourage all sponsoring organizations, especially those that are attempting to develop a community coalition, to consider having our trainers meet with potential participants **prior** to holding a workshop. We find that this step not only relieves fears and helps answer many questions, but it also greatly increases the effectiveness of the workshop. Also, a preliminary trainer visit is an excellent opportunity to have The People's Institute do some of the encouraging, convincing, and "selling" that you would have to do otherwise.

STEP 6 — CONSIDER THE FINANCES
EXPENSES
Workshop Fee

The basic fee for a two and a half day Undoing Racism Workshop is set on a sliding scale based upon ability to pay. Call The People's Institute for details regarding your situation. (Note: A non-refundable 15% deposit is required in order to reserve a workshop date. The balance is due in full upon completion of the workshop.)

Trainer Expenses

An Undoing Racism Workshop requires a minimum of two, and preferably three, trainers from The People's Institute. Workshop hosts cover trainer expenses, including:

*   Round-trip transportation to and from the workshop site. (We always work to keep this cost as low as possible. Advance air reservations and your assistance with local transportation are key factors.)

*   Meals during the course of the workshop.

*   Private rooms. (Simple accommodations are fine.)

Accommodations

*   A large meeting room to hold the workshop in.

*   Overnight accommodations for workshop participants. (This expense can vary greatly depending on

94

the type of accommodations desired and whether or not participants can return to their homes each night.)

Meals

We usually recommend that continental breakfasts, simple lunches, and snacks be provided at the workshop site. Suppers may be provided at the site, or participants may choose to go out. Again, this expense can vary greatly depending on the needs and interests of the group.

Other Possible Expenses

* Preliminary/Follow-up Consultations
* Publicity
* Child Care
* Newsprint, Markers, *etc.*

INCOME

Grants

General financial support to underwrite the cost of an Undoing Racism Workshop can be sought from:

* The organizations that are actually hosting the workshop.

* Local churches, community organizations, businesses, or other groups that are willing to invest in the work of undoing racism.

* Foundations. (We can provide leads about potential funding sources.)

Scholarship Donations

Individuals who are committed to the work of undoing racism (especially those who might not be able to attend the workshop) can make scholarship donations so that others can afford to attend.

Registration Fees

After all other funding sources are considered, registration fees can be calculated to cover the balance of the workshop expense. To determine registration fees, we suggest a sliding scale formula. (Please note: unless prior arrangements are made with The People's

Institute, Undoing Racism Workshops are to have no less than 10 and no more than 40 participants.)
 Total Expected Expenses

_____

 Total Expected Funding Support —

_____

 Total Registration Fees Needed =

_____

 _____ Persons at $_____ (Full Fee)

_____

 _____ Persons at $_____ (Half Fee) +

_____

 _____ Persons at $_____ (Nominal Fee)+

_____

 Total Registration Fees Expected =

_____

STEP 7 — SET A WORKSHOP DATE

Once your organization decides that it wants to host an Undoing Racism Workshop, potential dates can be discussed with the institute. The People's Institute will secure a workshop date upon receipt of a completed contract and the non-refundable 15% deposit.

STEP 8 — MEET WITH THE TRAINERS

At some point before the scheduled workshop date, a meeting (or conference call) is held with The People's Institute trainers and those hosting the workshop. The purpose of this meeting is to clarify needs, discuss expectations, establish goals, and develop an agreement for working together. Depending on the circumstances, some groups may find it helpful to take this step before committing to hosting a workshop.

STEP 9 — MAKE WORKSHOP ARRANGEMENTS PARTICIPANTS

Please be sure that all participants are aware of:
*   **The basic contents and purpose of the Undoing Racism Workshop.** Each participant should be

given a set of our brochures before the date of the workshop.

   *   **The basic commitment they are making.** See "The Training Commitment" in our brochure about the workshop. Note especially the agreement to be present for the entire time of the workshop.

   *   **The cultural sharing time.** Participants will appreciate advance notice of this opportunity to share.

   *   **The workshop schedule.** A typical Undoing Racism Workshop runs on a schedule similar to this one. Check with trainers for details.

Day 1:	7 PM - 10 PM	1st Session
Day 2:	9 AM - 12 PM	2nd Session
	12 PM - 1 PM	Lunch
	1 PM - 5 PM	3rd Session
	5 PM - 7 PM	Supper
	7 PM - 9 PM	Cultural Sharing
Day 3:	9 AM - 12 PM	4th Session
	12 PM - 1 PM	Lunch
	1 PM - 4 PM	5th Session

THE MEETING ROOM

Please be sure that the meeting room has:

   *   Adequate space for the entire group (10-40 people) to sit in a large circle.

   *   A sufficient number of comfortable chairs. (Participants are seated for most of the workshop.)

   *   Appropriate lighting.

   *   A comfortable temperature.

   *   Space to post newsprint.

   *   Limited noise distractions (*e.g.*: phones, fans, kitchens, traffic, music, other groups meeting, *etc.*)

SUPPLIES

Please be sure to supply the following items:

   *   Newsprint Pad (and Easel, if possible)

   *   Markers

   *   Masking Tape

* Blackboard
* Chalk & Eraser
* Paper and Pencils for participants
* Audio Cassette Player

PUBLICITY

Please note that all announcements of the Undoing Racism Workshop (press releases, ads, brochures, flyers, *etc.*) must be reviewed by The People's Institute staff **BEFORE** being released to the general public. We can provide sample materials that may be of assistance.

OTHER TASKS

* Registration
* Housing
* Meals
* Coffee & Snack Table
* Special Needs Accommodations
* Child Care
* Airport Shuttle
* Map/directions for workshop participants from out of town

FOR MORE INFORMATION. . .

About The People's Institute and the Undoing Racism Workshop, please contact:

The People's Institute for Survival and Beyond
1444 North Johnson Street
New Orleans, LA 70116
(504) 944-2354

APPENDIX C
THE CORE TRAINERS

Rev. David Billings

A native of McComb, Mississippi, David graduated with honors from the University of Mississippi in 1968, and in 1985 he graduated with a Master of Divinity degree from New York Theological Seminary. David is a United Methodist minister and has worked in church-related community projects for over 20 years. In 1976 he was awarded a certificate of merit for work against racism by the National Alliance Against Racism and Political Oppression. David is the director of the Greater New Orleans Urban Ministries (an ecumenical ministry) and co-founder of European Dissent, a group of white people combatting racism in New Orleans. Currently, David works as an independent consultant and serves as a member of the St. Thomas/Irish Channel Consortium.

Rev. Daniel Buford

While serving as campus minister at the University of Cincinnati, Dan led the organizing effort against turning a public school in a Black neighborhood into a military academy. Dan has served as coordinator of the Cincinnati Draft Information Service, director of Black Campus Ministries, co-founder of the 3rd World Caucus of Clergy and Laity Concerned, co-founder of the Committee Against Registration and the Draft, and director of the Ecumenical Peace Institute in Berkeley, CA. Dan has been a trainer/consultant to numerous church, community, and campus groups across the country in the areas of racism and militarism, and he is currently working on a book on linguistic racism. Dan is also a sculptor and the author of *Feet of Clay in Black America.*

Diana Dunn

Active in peace movements and community organizing since the late 1960s, Diana taught microbiology at Wright State University where she developed an innovative interdisciplinary program for medical technical students. Diana served as director of Help Us Make A Nation (HUMAN) and has conducted numerous workshops on racism for church, community, and women's groups. Currently, Diana is deputy director of the People's Institute for Survival and Beyond, she is active in her community with the Committee to Save Louis Armstrong Park, and she leads a local group of Euro-Americans seeking ways to break out of the "gatekeeper role" in this country's institutionalized culture of racism.

Barbara Major

For over 20 years, Barbara has been active in southern organizing, particularly with low-income women and children. She has also worked as a social worker for the state of Louisiana and as a military sergeant and Personal Records Specialist. In 1976, Barbara was an organizer with Advocates for Juvenile Justice where she worked to develop alternatives to incarceration for juvenile offenders. She then worked as director of the Louisiana Hunger Coalition and eventually took a staff position at the national office of Bread for the World. Barbara was co-founder and director of the Louisiana Survival Coalition, a broad-based advocacy and litigation project for empowerment of minorities and the poor. She was also appointed by the Mayor of New Orleans as Director of Human Relations. Barbara now works with Connective Ministries, a faith-based community group providing technical assistance to church and community organizations throughout the South. Currently, she is an independent consultant and remains active in the New Orleans community.